# Massachusetts

by the Capstone Press
Geography Department

CAPSTONE PRESS
MANKATO, MINNESOTA

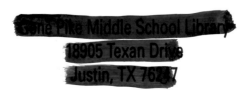

# C A P S T O N E  P R E S S
## 818 North Willow Street • Mankato, MN 56001

*Library of Congress Cataloging-in-Publication Data*
    Massachusetts/by the Capstone Press Geography Department
    p. cm.--(One Nation)
    Includes bibliographical references and index.
    Summary: Gives an overview of the state of Massachusetts, including its
    history, geography, people, and living conditions.
    ISBN 1-56065-437-6
    1. Massachusetts--Juvenile literature. [1. Massachusetts.]
    I. Capstone Press. Geography Dept. II. Series.
F64.3.M37 1996
974.4--dc20

                                        96-25567
                                          CIP
                                           AC

Photo credits
Massachusetts Division of Tourism, 4, 5 (left).
Unicorn/Aneal Vohra, 5 (right).
Archive Photos, 6.
Kay Shaw, 8, 18, 26, 34.
James Rowan, 10, 16, 22, 30.
G. Alan Nelson, 15.
Root Resources, cover 21, 25, 28, 32, 36.

# Table of Contents

Words in **boldface** type in the text are defined
in the Glossary in the back of this book.

# *Fast Facts about Massachusetts*

**State Flag**

**Location**: In the northeastern United States, along the Atlantic Ocean
**Size**: 8,686 square miles (22,583 square kilometers)

**Population**: 6,016,425 (1990 United States Census Bureau figures)
**Capital**: Boston
**Date admitted to the Union**: February 6, 1788; the sixth state

**Chickadee**

**Mayflower**

**Largest cities**: Boston, Worcester, Springfield, Lowell, New Bedford, Cambridge, Brockton, Fall River, Quincy, Newton

**Nickname**: The Bay State
**State bird**: Chickadee
**State flower**: Mayflower
**State tree**: American elm
**State song**: "All Hail to Massachusetts," written by Arthur J. Marsh

**American elm**

**5**

*Chapter 1*

# The USS *Constitution*

The Charlestown Navy Yard lies on the Charles River. Many warships have been built at the yard. One old ship still sits there.

A sailor shows visitors around the ship. Below deck, heavy cannons point through the portholes.

This ship is the USS *Constitution*. It first sailed in 1797.

**Old Ironsides**

In 1803, the United States sent the *Constitution* to fight pirates in the Mediterranean Sea. The ship also fought against the British during the War of 1812.

**The USS *Constitution* first sailed in 1797.**

The oak planks in the *Constitution's* hull were too tough for enemy cannonballs. Sailors gave it the nickname Old Ironsides.

Old Ironsides is still a commissioned warship in the United States Navy. It is the oldest one in the world.

## Massachusetts Past and Present

Massachusetts has been important in American history. In 1620, the Pilgrims founded England's second American colony. It was called Plymouth. Shots at Lexington and Concord started the Revolutionary War in 1775.

Today, Boston is a great sports town. The Celtics play basketball in Boston Garden. The Bruins play hockey there. Fenway Park is home to baseball's Boston Red Sox. In nearby Foxboro, the Patriots play football. Each April, runners take part in the Boston Marathon.

Students from around the world attend Harvard University. Cape Cod and the Berkshire Hills attract thousands of visitors.

**A statue of Paul Revere stands near Boston's Old North Church.**

# Chapter 2

# The Land

Massachusetts is in the northeastern United States. It is one of the six New England states. Massachusetts covers 8,686 square miles (22,583 square kilometers). Only five states are smaller than Massachusetts.

The Atlantic Ocean borders Massachusetts to the east and southeast. The state has more than 1,500 miles (2,400 kilometers) of coastline. Massachusetts' lowest point is sea level at the coast.

## The Coastal Lowlands

The Coastal Lowlands cover eastern Massachusetts. Glaciers left hilly, rocky land there. The Blue Hills begin south of Boston.

**The Fort Pickering Lighthouse stands in Salem.**

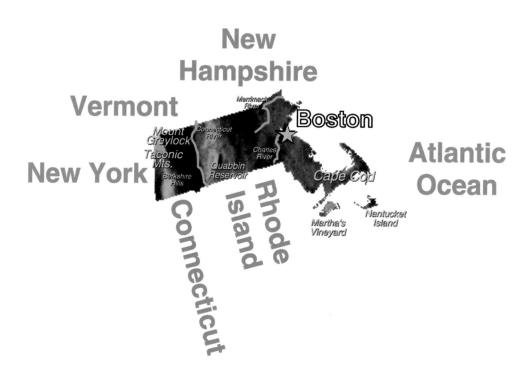

Ocean waves and glaciers created harbors. Gloucester, Boston, and New Bedford have deep harbors. Shipbuilding, shipping, and fishing developed in these towns.

Drifting sand and glacial rock formed Cape Cod. This peninsula has flat, sandy land. It stretches into the Atlantic Ocean. South of the cape is Nantucket Sound. Nantucket Island and Martha's Vineyard lie across the sound.

Short rivers run through the Coastal Lowlands. The Charles and Merrimack are main rivers. They both flow to the northeast. The Charles River empties into Boston Bay. The Merrimack River winds through northern Massachusetts.

## The Eastern Upland

The Eastern Upland covers the middle third of Massachusetts. There, the land becomes hillier. New Hampshire's White Mountains reach south into Massachusetts.

Massachusetts' largest lakes are in the Eastern Upland. The Quabbin and Wachusett reservoirs were formed by damming streams. These lakes provide water for the city of Boston.

## The Connecticut River Valley

The Connecticut River forms a broad valley in central Massachusetts. The state's most fertile soil lies there. Springfield is the largest city in the valley.

## Western Massachusetts

The Berkshire Hills stand in western Massachusetts. They are part of Vermont's Green Mountains. Mount Greylock is in the Berkshires. This is Massachusetts' highest point. Mount Greylock reaches 3,491 feet (1,047 meters) above sea level.

The Housatonic River flows through the Berkshires. Dairy cattle graze in the Berkshire Valley.

The Taconic Mountains rise to the west. They cross into New York and Vermont. The Hoosic River flows northwest through the Taconics into Vermont.

## Climate

Ocean breezes cool eastern Massachusetts in the summer and warm it in the winter. To the west, winters are colder. Summer temperatures are alike in the east and west.

Western Massachusetts gets more rain and snow. Hurricanes sometimes hit the Massachusetts coast.

**Massachusetts has many trees. About 60 percent of the state is wooded.**

## Wildlife

Foxes, rabbits, and poisonous timber rattlesnakes live in the Berkshire Hills. Beavers live in streams and lakes. Herons, seagulls, cranes, and terns live on coastal beaches.

Bass, trout, and perch swim in the state's lakes and ponds. Clams, lobsters, and oysters live in coastal waters.

# Chapter 3

# The People

With more than 6 million people, Massachusetts ranks 13th among the states. Massachusetts is one of the most urban states. Nearly 100 percent of Massachusetts' people live in cities and towns.

Bay Staters also live close together. There are 693 Bay Staters per square mile (267 per square kilometer). Only Rhode Island and New Jersey have more people per square mile.

Almost 90 percent of Bay Staters are white. Many of their ancestors were English colonists. The English founded many Massachusetts cities in the 1600s. They include Plymouth, Salem, and Boston.

**An actor portraying a settler makes clapboard at Plimoth Plantation. The Pilgrims settled Plymouth colony in 1620.**

Quincy Market is near Faneuil Hall in downtown Boston.

## European Immigrants

Boston has attracted many European immigrants. In the 1840s, a wave of Irish families came to Boston. They were escaping the potato famine. The Irish gained great political power. From 1929 to 1993, Irish Americans were mayors of Boston. Many Irish Americans live in Boston's North End.

In the early 1900s, more immigrants came from Italy, Poland, Portugal, and Greece.

Other cities in eastern Massachusetts also have large ethnic neighborhoods. Charleston has a large Irish population. Many Portuguese live in Fall River, New Bedford, and Provincetown.

## African Americans

African Americans make up 5 percent of the state's population. Boston has the state's largest African-American population. Boston's African-American neighborhoods include Roxbury and Dorchester.

Many African Americans came to Massachusetts as slaves. In 1780, Massachusetts abolished slavery.

Later, Massachusetts became the center of the abolitionist movement. Abolitionists wanted to outlaw slavery everywhere in the United States. They helped southern slaves escape to freedom.

More African Americans came to Massachusetts in the early 1900s. They hoped to find jobs in the state's factories.

## Hispanic Americans

Almost 5 percent of Bay Staters are Hispanic. Many of them came from Mexico, Puerto Rico, and Cuba. Hispanics speak Spanish or have Spanish-speaking ancestors.

Recent trouble in Central America brought other Hispanics to Massachusetts. They came from Guatemala, Honduras, Nicaragua, and Panama.

## Asian Americans

Asian Americans make up more than 2 percent of the state's population. A large Chinese community lives in Boston. Others have come from India, Japan, Korea, and the Philippines.

Since the 1970s, many Southeast Asians have moved to Massachusetts. Others are from Vietnam, Laos, and Thailand. Many Cambodian families settled in Lowell.

## Native Americans

About 12,000 Native Americans live in Massachusetts. The Wampanoag Indians are the major tribe. They live mainly on Cape Cod and Martha's Vineyard.

In 1987, the United States government granted them $4.5 million. With it, they regained 475 acres (190 hectares) of land.

**The Gloucester Fishermen's Memorial honors fishermen who have died at sea.**

THEY THAT GO
DOWN TO THE SEA
IN SHIPS
▲ ▲ ▲
1623 — 1923

# Chapter 4

# Massachusetts History

People have lived in Massachusetts at least 7,000 years. In the 1500s, about 30,000 Algonquins lived there. They included the Wampanoag, Pawtuxet, and Nipmuc.

## Explorers and Native Americans

In 1498, John Cabot sailed to North America from England. He claimed North America for the king of England. Samuel de Champlain claimed the same land for France in 1605. Native Americans traded with both the French and the English.

By 1620, only 7,000 Native Americans lived in Massachusetts. Many had died of diseases brought by the Europeans.

**The Mayflower II is a replica of the Pilgrims' ship.**

## English Colonists

In the 1600s, many English people wanted religious freedom. Two English groups found this freedom in Massachusetts. The Pilgrims settled Plymouth Colony in 1620. In 1630, the Puritans founded the Massachusetts Bay Colony. This colony was at Boston.

In 1691, the English king formed the colony of Massachusetts. The king controlled all of Massachusetts. By 1732, England had 13 colonies in North America.

## The Revolutionary War

In the 1760s, England began taxing the colonists more heavily. The colonists protested. English troops were sent to Massachusetts.

In 1775, colonial militias at Lexington and Concord fought the English. The Revolutionary War (1775-1783) had started.

The English were forced from Massachusetts in March of 1776. On July 4, the 13 colonies declared independence from England.

**Actors portray British soldiers in the Revolutionary War.**

## The State of Massachusetts

In 1783, a treaty ended the war. The United States became an independent nation. American leaders wrote the United States Constitution in 1787. Massachusetts ratified the Constitution in 1788. It became the sixth state of the Union.

Massachusetts grew rich from overseas trade. The state also became a manufacturing center. By

1860, Massachusetts led the nation in making textiles and shoes.

## The Civil War

The southern states left the Union. They formed the Confederate States of America. This led to the Civil War (1861-1865).

An issue of the war was slavery. The Union opposed it. The Confederacy allowed it. Many Bay Staters helped slaves escape to Canada.

Massachusetts' factories made uniforms, weapons, and ships for the Union. About 150,000 Massachusetts soldiers helped the Union win the war.

## Manufacturing Growth and Problems

After the war, the state's factories grew. Factory jobs attracted thousands of people from other nations.

Many factory workers labored long hours for low pay. In 1912, textile workers in Lawrence went on strike. The strike brought some improvements for workers.

**The Massachusetts State House in Boston has a gold dome.**

**Walden Pond was made famous by Henry David Thoreau. He lived in a cabin near the pond and wrote _Walden_.**

## World Wars and the Great Depression

During World War I (1914-1918), Massachusetts' factories produced ammunition, guns, and ships. About 200,000 Bay Staters served their country.

After the war, many Massachusetts businesses moved to the South. Labor was cheaper there. Many Bay Staters lost their jobs.

The Great Depression (1929-1939) made matters worse. By 1931, less than half of Massachusetts' workers had full-time jobs.

The United States entered World War II (1939-1945) in 1941. Once again, Bay Staters built ships and made weapons.

## Recent Changes and Challenges

The economy of Massachusetts changed in the 1950s. Electronic equipment and computers replaced heavy industry. The tourist industry also grew. New hotels popped up on Cape Cod. Ski resorts opened in the Berkshires.

Massachusetts has fought many problems. Bay Staters have worked to integrate housing and public schools. Lawmakers passed tough laws to clean Massachusetts' air and water.

A recession in the 1990s hurt Massachusetts' workers. Companies went out of business. People lost their jobs.

Massachusetts' leaders are trying to solve these problems. They want Massachusetts to be a great place to live and work.

# *Chapter 5*
# Massachusetts Business

Service industries make up the largest part of Massachusetts' economy. They include health care, education, banking, and insurance. Trade, government work, and tourism are other important Massachusetts services.

Manufacturing ranks second in Massachusetts. Agriculture and fishing play smaller parts in the economy.

## Service Industries

Boston is the center of Massachusetts' service industry. World-famous hospitals and medical research centers are there. Headquarters for two of the nation's largest banks are there, too. The city is home to many large insurance companies.

**The Minuteman statue in Lexington is a major tourist spot.**

**About half the country's cranberries are grown in Massachusetts.**

Harvard University is in nearby Cambridge. The Massachusetts Institute of Technology is there, too. Thousands of people study, teach, and do research at these schools. Researchers provide information for Massachusetts' software and computer industries.

Each year, tourism adds about $6 billion to Massachusetts' economy. The state's hotels, resorts, and restaurants receive much of this money.

## Manufacturing

Massachusetts has been a manufacturing state for almost 200 years. Some factories make shoes, textiles, and paper. Others make computers, electrical equipment, and scientific instruments. Automobiles, processed foods, and chemicals are other manufactured products.

## Agriculture

Most of Massachusetts' soil is too rocky for farming. Massachusetts' farmers do grow flowers, apples, sweet corn, and tobacco. They also grow about half the nation's cranberries.

Dairy farming is important in the Connecticut Valley. Farmers also raise poultry and beef cattle.

## Fishing

Massachusetts is a leading fishing state. Large fishing fleets anchor at Gloucester, Boston, and New Bedford. Their crews catch flounder, cod, scallops, and perch. Clams, crabs, and lobsters are other Massachusetts fishing products.

# Chapter 6

# Seeing the Sights

Massachusetts has many interesting sights. Natural sights include the Berkshires and Cape Cod. Boston, Salem, and Plymouth have many historic places. Massachusetts' small towns and country roads have something for everyone.

## Boston

Boston is the largest city in Massachusetts and in New England. It is also Massachusetts' capital. The State Capitol is in downtown Boston. It is across from Boston Commons. This is the oldest park in the nation.

Buildings from the Revolutionary War still stand in Boston. Visitors follow the Freedom Trail to see them.

The Old North Church is one of these buildings. In April 1775, signals flashed from the steeple. They

**Old Sturbridge Village shows country life in the 1830s.**

**The Cape Cod National Seashore has many miles of beaches.**

warned that the English were heading to Lexington and Concord. Paul Revere rode ahead to warn the people in Lexington.

Faneuil Hall was a meeting place even before the revolution. Today, its lower floor has shops and restaurants. The second floor is still used for public meetings.

Visitors can also walk along the Black Heritage Trail. This tour highlights African-American history in Boston.

Boston also has many modern attractions. The John Hancock Tower is more than 60 stories high. This is New England's tallest building. The Computer Museum shows how computers and robots work. Visitors can walk through a two-story computer.

## Northeastern Massachusetts

Far northwest of Boston is Lowell. Textile mills bloomed there in the 1800s. Today, some of these mills are museums. They have working looms. Computer factories now provide work for the town.

Gloucester lies to the east. It is on the Atlantic Ocean. Catching and packing fish keep the townspeople busy. The Gloucester Fisherman statue stands at the harbor. It honors fishermen who died at sea.

Salem is another coastal town. It is south of Gloucester. In 1692, the Salem witchcraft trials were held. Nineteen men and women were hanged as witches. The Witch Dungeon Museum shows one of the trials.

## Cape Cod

Provincetown sits at the tip of Cape Cod. Provincetown was once a whaling town. Today, people take boat trips to watch the whales.

The Cape Cod National Seashore runs along the cape's northern arm. It includes many miles of beaches and sand dunes.

Hyannis Port is on the cape's southern shore. Many artists and writers have summer homes there. Ferries run from Hyannis Port to Martha's Vineyard and Nantucket.

## Central Massachusetts

Central Massachusetts has rolling hills and fields. Fishing boats sail on its lakes and ponds.

Worcester is in the eastern part of this region. It is Massachusetts' second largest city. This town has 10 colleges and universities. The Higgins Armory Museum is there, too. Visitors can try on pieces of armor.

To the southwest is Sturbridge. Old Sturbridge Village shows country life in the 1830s.

Springfield is west of Sturbridge. Basketball fans stop there to visit the Naismith Memorial Basketball Hall of Fame. James Naismith invented basketball in 1891 in Springfield.

## Western Massachusetts

People visit the Berkshire Hills in all seasons. Skiers go down the slopes in winter. Lenox holds the Tanglewood Music Festival each summer. This is the Boston Symphony's summer home.

Stockbridge is to the south. The Norman Rockwell Museum is there. It has the largest collection of Rockwell's original paintings.

The Mohawk Trail is in northwestern Massachusetts. This road is especially beautiful in the fall. Drivers enjoy the changing colors of the leaves.

# Massachusetts Time Line

**5000 B.C.**—The first people arrive in Massachusetts.

**1000 B.C.**—The Algonquins arrive in Massachusetts.

**1498**—John Cabot claims North America for England.

**1620**—The Pilgrims land in Massachusetts and build a colony at Plymouth.

**1630**—The Puritans found the Massachusetts Bay Colony and begin the city of Boston.

**1691**—Massachusetts colonies are united as the Massachusetts Colony under England's control.

**1692**—Witchcraft trials are held in Salem.

**1770**—English troops open fire on colonists, causing the Boston Massacre.

**1773**—In what became known as the Boston Tea Party, colonists dump tea in Boston Harbor to protest the tax on tea.

**1775**—Colonial militias fight English troops in Lexington and Concord, starting the Revolutionary War.

**1788**—Massachusetts becomes the sixth state.

**1815**—Francis Cabot Lowell opens a textile mill in Waltham.

**1831**—In Boston, William Lloyd Garrison begins printing *The Liberator*, an antislavery newspaper.

**1876**—Alexander Graham Bell invents the telephone in Boston.

**1897**—Boston opens the nation's first subway.

**1912**—Textile workers go on strike in Lawrence.

**1927**—Two Italian immigrants, Nicola Sacco and Bartolomeo Vanzetti, are executed for committing murder during a robbery in Braintree.

**1959**—The *Long Beach*, the first nuclear-powered surface ship in the United States Navy, is launched in Quincy harbor.

**1960**—Massachusetts senator John F. Kennedy is elected president of the United States.

**1974**—A federal court orders busing to achieve desegregation of Boston's schools.

**1988**—Governor Michael Dukakis of Massachusetts loses the United States presidential election to George Bush, who was born in Milton.

**1993**—Thomas M. Menino becomes the first Italian-American mayor of Boston.

# Famous Bay Staters

**John Adams** (1735-1826) Lawyer who became the second president of the United States (1797-1801); born in present-day Quincy.

**John Quincy Adams** (1767-1848) Son of John Adams; became the sixth president of the United States; born in present-day Quincy.

**Samuel Adams** (1722-1803) Cousin of John Adams; organized the Boston Tea Party; born in Boston.

**Susan B. Anthony** (1820-1906) Worked for women's right to vote; born in Adams.

**Edward Brooke** (1919- ) Politician who became the first African-American senator from Massachusetts (1967-1979).

**George Bush** (1924- ) Businessman and politician who became the 41st president of the United States (1989-1993); born in Milton.

**Emily Dickinson** (1830-1886) One of the great poets in American literature; born in Amherst.

**W. E. B. DuBois** (1868-1963) Civil rights leader who helped found the National Association for the Advancement of Colored People; born in Great Barrington.

**Benjamin Franklin** (1706-1790) Inventor, diplomat, and author; helped write the Declaration of Independence and the Constitution; born in Boston.

**Nathaniel Hawthorne** (1804-1864) Author who wrote *The Scarlet Letter* and *The House of Seven Gables*; born in Salem.

**Winslow Homer** (1836-1910) Painter who created famous sailing scenes; born in Boston.

**Theodore Seuss Geisel** (1904-1991) Author and illustrator who created the Dr. Seuss books; born in Springfield.

**John F. Kennedy** (1917-1963) Politician who became the 35th president of the United States (1961-1963); born in Brookline.

**Metacom (King Philip)** (?-1676) Wampanoag chief; led raids on English settlers that became known as King Philip's War (1675-1678).

**Anne Sexton** (1928-1974) Pulitzer Prize-winning poet; born in Newton.

**Squanto** (1585-1622) Pawtuxet Indian who helped the settlers in the Plymouth Colony.

# Glossary

**abolitionist**—a person who worked to outlaw slavery in the 1800s

**ancestor**—a person from whom one is descended

**colony**—a group of people who settle in a different land but remain under control of their native country

**commission**—to be officially in use and ready for action

**ethnic**—of a group with a common culture

**glacier**—huge sheets of slow-moving ice

**immigrant**—a person who comes to another country to settle

**integrate**—to bring people of different races together

**manufacturing**—the making of products

**militia**—citizens who are not professional soldiers called to serve in the armed forces during emergencies

**peninsula**—land bordered by water on three
   sides
**ratify**—to officially approve a law or document
**recession**—a time when the economy slows
   down
**reservoir**—a lake or pond where water is
   collected and stored
**strike**—to stop work and demand better pay or
   working conditions
**textile**—cloth or fibers used to make cloth
**urban**—relating to cities

# To Learn More

**Fradin, Dennis Brindell**. *Massachusetts*. From Sea to Shining Sea. Chicago: Children's Press, 1991.

**Kent, Deborah**. *Massachusetts*. America the Beautiful. Chicago: Children's Press, 1987.

**Lovett, Sarah**. *Unique New England: A Guide to the Region's Quirks, Charisma, and Character*. Santa Fe, N.M.: John Muir Publications, 1994.

**Warner, J. F**. *Massachusetts*. Hello USA. Minneapolis: Lerner Publications, 1994.

# Internet Sites

**City.Net Massachusetts**
http://www.city.net/countries/united_states/massachusetts
**Travel.org-Massachusetts**
http://travel.org/massachu
**Commonwealth of Massachusetts**
http://www.magnet.state.ma.us/
**Massachusetts Tourist Information**
http://www.masstourist.com/

# Useful Addresses

**Cape Cod National Seashore**
South Wellfleet, MA 02663

**Naismith Memorial Basketball Hall of Fame**
1150 West Columbus Avenue
Springfield, MA 01101

**Paul Revere House**
19 North Square
Boston, MA 02113

**Marine Museum at Fall River**
70 Water Street
Fall River, MA 02721

**Old Sturbridge Village**
1 Old Sturbridge Village Road
Sturbridge, MA 01566

# Index